RON MILLER

ASTEROIDS, COMETS, AND METEORS

WORLDS BEYOND

TFCB TWENTY-FIRST CENTURY BOOKS   MINNEAPOLIS

Dedicated to Olivia Olsen

Illustrations and text copyright © 2006 by Ron Miller
Photographs courtesy of NASA

Twenty-First Century Books
A division of Lerner Publishing Group
241 First Avenue North
Minneapolis, Minnesota 55401 U.S.A.

Website address: www.lernerbooks.com

Library of Congress Cataloging-in-Publication Data

Miller, Ron, 1947–
    Asteroids, comets, and meteors / Ron Miller.
    p.   cm. — (Worlds beyond)
    Summary: Chronicles the formation of the solar system, particularly how asteroids,
comets, and meteors were formed, and relates how astronomers learn about the existence
and characteristics of these bodies. Includes bibliographical references and index.
    ISBN 0-7613-2363-5 (lib. bdg.)
    1. Asteroids—Juvenile literature. 2. Comets—Juvenile literature. 3. Meteors—Juvenile
literature. [1. Asteroids. 2. Comets. 3. Meteors. 4. Astronomy—History. 5. Solar system.]
I. Title.
QB651 .M55 2003
523.5—dc21   2003010410

Manufactured in the United States of America
1 2 3 4 5 6 – DP – 11 10 09 08 07 06

CONTENTS

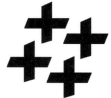 

Astronomical symbols for the asteroids and a comet

During the formation of our solar system, a knot of nebular dust and gas collapsed, and a proto-planetary disk formed.

CHAPTER ONE

BUILDING A SOLAR SYSTEM

After a house has been built there are always a lot of leftovers: bricks, pieces of wood, cardboard, glass and plastic, empty boxes, loose nails, and whatnot. The same thing happened when the solar system formed. Not all of the material in the vast cloud of dust and gas, which eventually became the solar system, was used up when forming the Sun and planets. There was a lot of debris left over: ice and metal and rock. This book is about those leftovers.

The Birth of the Solar System

The Sun and planets formed about 4.5 billion years ago from an enormous cloud of dust and gas. The cloud was large enough for the gravitation of its individual particles to start the cloud contracting and then to maintain the **contraction**. Once this process began, the cloud shrank to a millionth of its original size very quickly.

As it grew smaller and denser, it began to rotate, which caused it to flatten into a disk, just as a pizza maker will make his dough flatten into a thin disk by spinning it rapidly. The center of the **protoplanetary disk** of dust and gas grew hotter and denser and eventually formed a **protostar**—a ball of gas that's not quite hot enough for nuclear reactions to begin.

As the center of the cloud continued to become denser, its gravity increased. Soon the core was hot enough to glow a dull red within the dark cloud. It was finally hot enough for a nuclear reaction to begin—perhaps only a few thousand years after the cloud first began to condense—and when this happened, the protostar became a **star**. The increased amount of heat it produced created an outward pressure that resisted the collapsing dust and gas, and the collapse came to a halt.

Within the cloud, tiny particles of dust collided and stuck together, forming little clumps of material, in a process called **accretion**. As these clumps, called **planetesimals**, grew in size, their gravity increased, and they attracted even more particles. Most of the early collisions were relatively gentle, so the planetesimals didn't become fragmented. Soon these clumps of dust grew to the size of rocks, then boulders, and then **asteroids** miles across.

As the planetesimals grew larger they began to move faster, and the collisions between them became more violent. It was like the difference between people bumping into one another in a crowd and automobiles crashing together in a demolition derby. Now, instead of accreting and growing ever larger, some of the planetesimals shattered into pieces. The few planetesimals large enough to survive the collisions grew even larger, devouring the debris from the smaller objects. Eventually, they grew to be the size of planets. In fact, they *became* planets.

The heat from the new star, the Sun, prevented ice from forming on the planets closest to it. Mercury, Venus, Earth, and Mars were therefore formed mostly from metals and rocky mate-

rials. At the distance of Jupiter and beyond, plenty of ice remained, and those planets were created mostly from a mixture of ice, rock, and metal.

The newly formed planets, however, did not sweep up all of the material in the original cloud of dust and gas. The space between Mars and Jupiter remained filled with rocky, metallic planetesimals—thousands upon thousands of them—that were prevented from accreting into planet-sized objects because of the tugging of Jupiter's powerful gravity. And in the vast region beyond Pluto, swarms of uncounted billions of icy objects were left over; this is all that remains of the original primordial cloud.

MINIATURE WORLDS

Many thousands of years ago, people observing the sky noticed that five stars seemed to be very unusual. All of the other stars remained in the same positions relative to one another from night to night, month to month, and year to year, but these other five stars *moved*. Because they appeared to wander across the sky, they were called *planets*, from the Greek word *planetes*, which means "wanderer." They were each named after Roman gods: Mercury was named for the messenger of the gods because it was the swiftest-moving. Venus was named for the goddess of love and beauty because it was the most beautiful. Mars was named for the god of war because of its red color. Jupiter was named for the king of the gods because of its size, and Saturn was named for the god of time and destiny because it was the slowest moving. Other than their unusual habit of moving through the sky, and that they were among the brightest stars, there didn't seem to be anything particularly special about the planets. That is, until an Italian scientist named Galileo Galilei pointed a new invention called a telescope at the night sky.

On those nights in 1610, Galileo discovered that the planets weren't just unusual stars—they were *worlds*, perhaps very much like our own Earth. Venus, he found, showed phases like those of the Moon, Mars was a ruddy globe with dusky markings, and, most amazing of all, Jupiter had four moons of its own circling it, like a miniature solar system.

Soon, many other astronomers were looking at the sky with telescopes, and as the years passed and telescopes grew larger and more powerful, more and more discoveries were made about the planets. Other discoveries were made using pen, ink, and paper as mathematicians worked out the complex laws that govern the movement of the planets.

At about the same time that Galileo was making his observations, the German mathematician Johannes Kepler published three laws of planetary motion that described how the planets moved in their orbits. Nearly eighty years later, in England, Isaac Newton discovered the laws of gravity and motion that explained *how* the Sun kept the planets in their orbits. It seemed to many scientists that the solar system was like a giant machine that worked according to strict, predictable mathematical rules.

A Strange "Law"

A strange mathematical relationship among the orbits of the planets was discovered in 1766 by the German astronomer Johann Daniel Titius. His colleague, Johann Bode, popularized it in 1778, and it soon became known as Bode's Rule. It works like this: Bode and Titius wrote down a series of 4s. Beneath the first 4 they placed a 0. Under the second 4 they placed a 3, then 6, 12, 24, etc., doubling the number each time. They added these pairs of numbers and then divided by ten. The result was a table something like this:

4	4	4	4	4	4	4	4	4
0	3	6	12	24	48	96	192	384
0.4	0.7	1.0	1.6	2.8	5.2	10.0	19.6	38.8

The astronomers noticed immediately that six of the numbers almost exactly matched the distances of the known planets from the Sun in **astronomical units** (**AU**s):

	MERCURY	VENUS	EARTH	MARS	?	JUPITER	SATURN
Predicted Distance	0.4	0.7	1.0	1.6	2.8	5.2	10.0
Actual Distance	0.39	0.72	1.0	1.52	?	5.2	9.5

Bode's Rule got a real boost when Uranus was discovered by William Herschel in 1781. The new planet fit into the chart almost perfectly. The rule showed that the distance from the Sun of the next planet beyond Saturn should be 19.6 AU. The actual distance of Uranus turned out to be 19.19.

Is Bode's Rule a real law of nature or just a mathematical coincidence? Most astronomers today believe that it is just a coincidence. After all, the rule is hardly perfect: There is no planet between Mars and Jupiter where Bode's Rule says there should be one, and there is a planet between Uranus and Pluto where the Rule says there should not be one. Also, most of the planets recently discovered circling stars outside our solar system don't appear to follow Bode's Rule.

And what about that question mark in the fifth position? Many astronomers, impressed with the accuracy of Bode's Rule, began searching for the planet they thought must exist in order to fill the fifth position.

In 1800 six astronomers met in Lilienthal, Germany, to determine a plan for tracking down the missing planet. Dubbed the "celestial police," they worked out a scheme where each one would be responsible for observing a certain part of the **ecliptic**, where the mysterious planet, if it existed at all, would most likely be found.

All of this seemed very organized and efficient, but while the Germans were making their plans an Italian astronomer named Giuseppe Piazzi, the director of the observatory at Palermo, Sicily, quietly stole their glory. Looking for **comets** on the night of January 1, 1801, he observed a tiny starlike object that moved from night to night. At first he thought it was a new comet, but suspected that it might be something much more exciting. He wrote to the German committee, but before they received his letter, the mysterious object had moved behind the Sun and could no longer be seen. Piazzi, however, had made enough observations to calculate the object's orbit, and it was clear that it was not a comet. Comets, Piazzi knew, had very **elliptical** orbits that carried them first far beyond Jupiter and then close to the Sun. This new object had a much more circular orbit—more like that of a planet.

Piazzi named the object Ceres, after the patron goddess of Sicily. Surely it was the predicted new planet: It was at exactly the distance predicted by Bode's Rule. Bode predicted a planet at 2.8

Giuseppe Piazzi

AU from the Sun, and Ceres orbited at 2.77. An almost perfect hit! But Ceres turned out to be something of a disappointment. It ended up to be less than 500 miles (800 km) wide, scarcely large enough to be called a real planet.

Just in case there might have been some error in Piazzi's observation—perhaps he was observing the wrong object—the celestial police continued their search. Sure enough, astronomer H. Olbers found yet another tiny world in 1802, which he named Pallas. Two more objects were discovered over the next five years: Juno in 1804 and Vesta in 1807. All were disappointingly small—in fact, none was larger than Ceres. Astraea, the fifth, which was

Astronomers have long disagreed about what to call the asteroids. The word *asteroid* itself is misleading, since it means "starlike." Although they do look like stars through a telescope, asteroids are, of course, nothing at all like stars. *Planetoid* is a far preferable term, though it has never quite caught on among non-astronomers, or even many astronomers for that matter. Most scientists seem to prefer *minor planet,* although just about everyone else continues to call them asteroids.

discovered in 1830, is only 100 miles (160 km) wide. They are all such tiny worlds that the term *minor planet* was coined to describe them, though most people call them *asteroids*, which means "star-like."

Although it took nearly thirty years to find the first five asteroids and another seventeen years before a sixth one was discovered, the floodgates had been opened. By 1890 the number grew to three hundred. Until then astronomers were searching for asteroids by laboriously gazing through telescopes. But in 1891, the German astronomer Max Wolf invented a new way to look for asteroids, which caused the number of asteroids being discovered every year to increase dramatically.

Wolf attached a camera to a telescope that was equipped with a clockwork mechanism, which allowed it to follow the stars as they moved across the sky. In the resulting photograph, the stars appeared as sharp points but an asteroid showed up as a streak of light. This is because an asteroid moves in relation to the fixed stars. Wolf's method was enormously successful, and he discovered a hundred new asteroids by himself. Today astronomers have cataloged several hundred thousand asteroids. One current estimate on the number of asteroids orbiting between Mars and Jupiter is 1.1 to 1.9 million.

When asteroids were first discovered, naming them seemed simple enough. Names from Greek and Roman mythology were used, just as they had been for the planets. But when the number of known asteroids began to grow into the hundreds and even thousands, naming all of them became a problem. An international committee of astronomers—the International Astronomical Union—was eventually created to set some rules for naming asteroids. The International Astronomical Union now oversees the naming of all bodies in space.

When an asteroid is first discovered, it is given a provisional number. When its orbit is understood well enough that its future position can be reliably predicted, it is given a permanent number and name. Thus, 243 Ida is the 243rd asteroid to be numbered (though not necessarily the 243rd to be discovered). Unlike the planets and moons, which have very strict rules about nomenclature, the asteroids can be named almost anything their discoverers choose, as long as they do so within ten years. But the names must be pronounceable and not more than 16 characters long.

We have asteroids named for relatives, schools, and friends. (Pets, for some reason, aren't allowed!) Some are named after scientists such as Darwin, Sagan, and Einstein; musicians from Bach, Mozart, and Beethoven to Elvis Presley, Enya, and Bruce Springsteen; places such as Antarctica and Buenos Aires; authors and poets such as Chaucer, Shakespeare, and Dickens; science fiction writers like Arthur C. Clarke, J.R.R. Tolkien, and Isaac Asimov. Some names are just funny, such as Mr. Spock and Hippo (to say nothing of Ekard, named by two graduates of Drake University who playfully spelled the name of their school backward). Most recently, some asteroids have been named for victims of the terrorist attacks on September 11, 2001.

NAMING ASTEROIDS

CHAPTER THREE

CHAPTER THREE

THE ASTEROID BELT

Of the hundreds of thousands of known asteroids, the vast majority of them—at least 98 percent—lie in the region between Mars and Jupiter known as the **asteroid belt**. This has become famous in science fiction, which gives the impression that the belt is a dense swarm of flying rocks and that any spaceship trying to pass through it would be in danger of being destroyed by a collision, like a ship trying to cross a dangerous reef. Although there are millions of asteroids in the belt, and at least 40,000 that are more than 0.5 mile (1 km) across, they are scattered over a vast area—some 10,000 trillion square miles (25.9 quadrillion km^2). It would be extremely rare for an asteroid to even come within sight of another one.

The asteroid belt itself is divided into distinct regions, with gaps between them where few if any asteroids can be found. These gaps were discovered in 1866 by an American astronomer named Daniel Kirkwood. His calculations revealed that the gaps were caused by the influence of Jupiter's gravity. The gaps occur

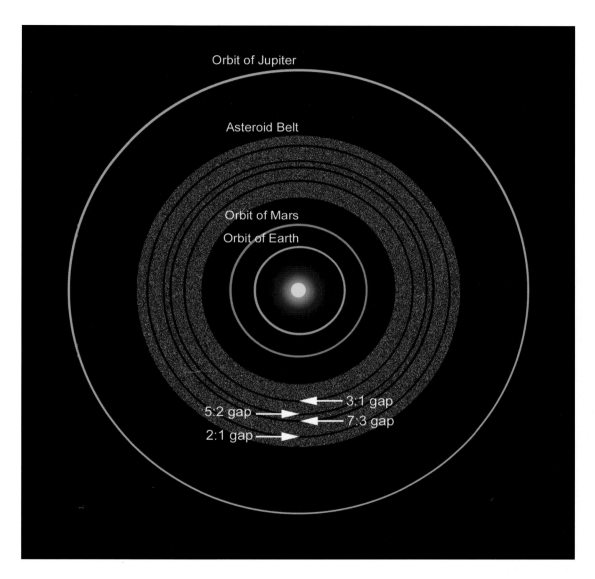

Orbit of Jupiter

Asteroid Belt

Orbit of Mars

Orbit of Earth

3:1 gap

5:2 gap

7:3 gap

2:1 gap

More than 90 percent of all asteroids are in the main asteroid belt that lies between the orbits of Mars and Jupiter. Kirkwood gaps are areas in the belt where asteroids would orbit in simple ratios to the orbit of Jupiter. Regular "kicks" from Jupiter's gravity gradually clear asteroids from these spaces.

The French mathematician Joseph Louis Lagrange discovered that when one body orbits another, such as a planet around the Sun or moons around a planet, there are five points of gravitational stability. Anything located in one of these points—called **Lagrangian points** in his honor—would tend to remain there. Only two of the five are permanently stable, the points called L4 and L5. These lie 60 degrees ahead of a planet in its orbit and 60 degrees behind. Jupiter has groups of asteroids orbiting at the two Lagrangian points just ahead of it and just behind it in its orbit. These groups are called **Trojan asteroids**. Mars also has at least three Trojan asteroids, but searches for Trojans associated with the other planets have been mostly unsuccessful.

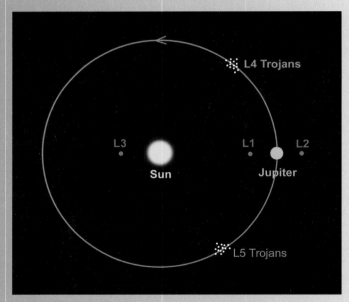

The five Lagrangian points are seen here in association with Jupiter's orbit. L4 and L5 are Jupiter's Trojan asteroids, which are in a permanent orbit.

when the orbit of an asteroid has a definite mathematical relationship with that of Jupiter. For instance, the ratio 3:1 means that every time the asteroid orbits three times around the Sun, Jupiter orbits once. Other important ratios include 5:2 and 2:1.

Each gap corresponds to one of these ratios. For example, every time an asteroid comes close to Jupiter in its orbit around the Sun, it will get a little "kick" from Jupiter's gravity. If the orbit of the asteroid is in some simple ratio to that of Jupiter, then these kicks come in a regular pattern. If the effect is that of speeding the asteroid up, it moves into a larger orbit, farther from the Sun. If the effect is that of slowing the asteroid down, it moves into a smaller orbit, closer to the Sun. The overall effect is that a space is cleared in the belt. These **Kirkwood gaps**, as they are now called, can also be found in Saturn's rings, where they are caused by the gravitational influence of the planet's large moons.

What Is an Asteroid?

Early astronomers thought that the asteroids were the remnants of an ancient planet that had been destroyed, perhaps as the result of a massive collision. Modern astronomers doubt this for several reasons. One reason is that the total mass of all the asteroids in the main asteroid belt has been estimated at less than 1/1000th of the mass of Earth. Indeed, if all asteroids that exist today, including those as small as 1 yard (0.9 m), were combined together, the resulting object would measure less than 810 to 930 miles (1,300 to 1,500 km) across. This is less than one third to one half the diameter of our Moon—not much of a planet. It is much more likely, astronomers think, that the asteroids are material that simply never coalesced into a single larger object in the first place.

The main asteroid belt today is probably only a small remnant of the material that once filled the solar system. In the early days, the region between Mars and Jupiter may have contained material equal to that of two to ten Earth masses. But gravitational perturbations from nearby Jupiter, as well as collisions among the planetesimals during the first 100 million years, prevented the formation of a large planet in the belt. Eventually most of the original material was either absorbed by the other planets in the solar system or blown out of the solar system by powerful **solar winds**—outrushing gases—from the newly formed Sun. Since today's asteroids are debris left over from the formation of the solar system—in other words, they are samples of the original planetesimals from which planets such as Earth and Mars were formed—scientists are very interested in them. They provide a glimpse into the early history of the solar system.

There were probably many large asteroids in the days of the early solar system. These large asteroids, or **protoplanets**, may have accumulated a great amount of internal heat. This heat was generated by the squeezing effect of gravitational collapse and by naturally radioactive elements. The heat caused denser metals to sink toward the middle of the asteroid (perhaps forming a metallic core like that of a planet), leaving the lighter rocky material in the outer layer. This is called **differentiation**. On some of the largest asteroids, internal heat formed **metamorphic rocks**, and volcanoes erupted.

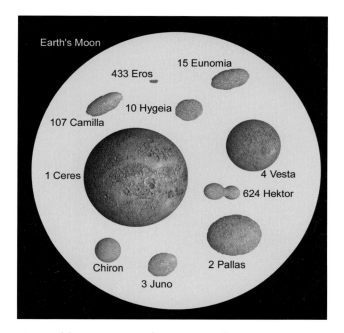

Several large asteroids compared in size to Earth's Moon

There are much fewer large asteroids now. The region between Mars and Jupiter might today contain only a few hundred large planetoids if the early asteroid belt was not a violent place. But as Jupiter grew into a giant planet, its increasing gravitational pull began to disturb the orbits of the nearest planetesimals. This caused more and more collisions to take place. The larger, differentiated protoplanets collided, shattering into smaller asteroids. Most of the present-day asteroid belt is composed of the remnants of the larger, original planetesimals.

Judging by the composition of some extraterrestrial objects that have landed on Earth—called **meteorites**—astronomers believe they are from the asteroid belt. It seems that asteroids are composed of three possible materials. Most of them, 92.8 percent, are made of **silicates**, 5.7 percent are made of iron and nickel, and the rest are a mix of metal, stone, and **carbon**-rich substances. Apparently some of them were formed from the outer, rocky crusts of the ancient planetesimals and some from their metallic cores.

The asteroids located close to Mars and Earth are usually composed of rocky minerals mixed with iron. On the other hand, the carbon-rich asteroids located closer to Jupiter are generally darker and redder. This is probably because they are farther from the Sun, and therefore there wasn't as much heat to drive away the lighter elements. These asteroids have a composition more like the primordial dust disk out of which the planets accreted some 4.5 billion years ago. Although it's unlikely that any asteroid in the main belt ever grew big enough to have the amount of gravity necessary to hold onto an atmosphere, minerals found in some objects suggest that liquid water may have been present.

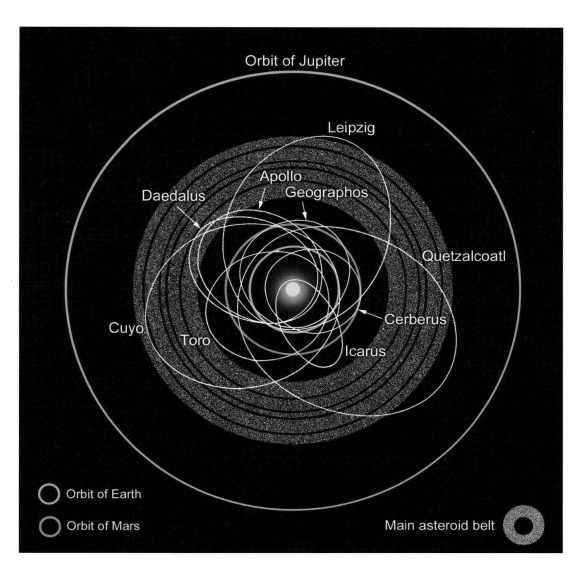

Orbit of Jupiter

Leipzig

Apollo

Daedalus

Geographos

Quetzalcoatl

Cerberus

Cuyo

Toro

Icarus

○ Orbit of Earth

○ Orbit of Mars

Main asteroid belt

The asteroid belt showing the orbits of several near-Earth asteroids (NEAs) or Earth-approachers: These asteroids—and many others like them—have highly eccentric orbits that swing close to Earth.

(21)

Interplanetary Traffic Jam

While most of the asteroids are neatly confined to the asteroid belt, the remaining 2 percent have wildly eccentric orbits, swinging from as far out as Jupiter to as close to the Sun as Mercury. When an asteroid gets closer to the Sun than Earth is, it has to cross Earth's orbit. This is where things become a little dangerous.

The orbits of an asteroid and Earth could cross in the same way that a highway and railroad tracks might meet at a grade crossing. If the asteroid and Earth were to meet at the crossing, the results would be as if a train and a car were to meet—but a billion times more catastrophic. Fortunately, the orbits of most asteroids that cross that of Earth resemble the way a highway and railroad meet at an overpass. Although the two paths cross, one passes over the other and they never come close to colliding.

Still, a collision between Earth and an asteroid is not impossible. It's happened many times in the past—it was the result of an impact with a relatively small asteroid that wiped out the dinosaurs—and there's little reason to think it won't happen again. The effect of the impact of even a small asteroid would be catastrophic, and a collision with a large one could spell the end of life on Earth as we know it.

There is a whole class of asteroids bearing the disturbing name of Earth-approachers. These are asteroids that come much closer to Earth than any others—sometimes closer than our own Moon. During the twentieth century astronomers found more than one hundred such bodies that approach close to Earth's orbit. They range in size from around 0.6 mile (1 km) to around 18 miles (30

In 1965, asteroid 1999 VP11 came within 18,591 miles (29,918 km) of our planet—much closer to Earth than the Moon, which is 238,600 miles (384,000 km) away. Even a small asteroid such as this one would cause catastrophic damage if it were to hit our planet.

km). Some astronomers think that all the large Earth-approachers have been found, but twenty-first century astronomers continue to find new ones at sizes smaller than a half mile to as small as 300 feet (91 m) or so.

Astronomers estimate that there are probably only about twenty objects larger than 3 miles (5 km) that actually could hit Earth. This would cause a global catastrophe, but the chances of one hitting our planet within even 1 million years are very low. Scientists base this estimate on how many giant impact **craters** exist on the Moon, Mars, and other worlds where erosion hasn't erased them. Knowing how old these worlds are gives scientists an idea of how often these impacts occur. It will probably be 10 or even 100 million years before an impact would occur. This is why astronomers say that the probability of a global catastrophic impact in any person's lifetime is quite small. However, it is not unlikely that in our lifetime a much smaller asteroid fragment could hit Earth and cause a localized, nuclear bomb–sized explosion in an inhabited area.

The asteroid Icarus has a highly eccentric orbit that swings as far away as 2 AU—farther from the Sun than the orbit of Mars—to as close to the Sun as 0.2 AU, which is nearer the Sun than Mercury. During the course of Icarus's year, the Sun, as seen from Icarus, would appear to change in size from half the diameter it appears from Earth to five times larger.

CHAPTER FOUR

EXPLORING ASTEROIDS

For years, astronomers had little interest in asteroids—in fact, they considered them a nuisance. "The vermin of the sky," one astronomer called them. "Ten thousand fleas on the black dog of night," in the words of a science fiction author. Astronomers trying to count stars found that asteroids made their work harder, and those trying to photograph stars found their photographic plates filled with irritating little streaks. It wasn't until fairly recently that astronomers decided that asteroids are in fact very interesting indeed.

To date, four main asteroids have been photographed close up: 951 Gaspra, 243 Ida, 253 Mathilde, and 433 Eros. The *Galileo* spacecraft studied Gaspra and Ida on its way to Jupiter, while the **NEAR** *Shoemaker* spacecraft visited Mathilde and Eros. A fifth asteroid, Braille, was photographed from a distance by the *Deep Space 1* spacecraft. (The *Stardust* spacecraft photographed the asteroid 5535 Annefrank in November 2002 when the *Stardust* was on its way to rendezvous with Comet Wild-2. It only did so, however, to check its imaging equipment. *Stardust* was too far from the asteroid to take any useful pictures of it. Tiny Annefrank is only about 2.5 miles [4 km] wide.)

The first of the asteroids to be observed close up was Gaspra, which *Galileo* flew past in 1991. *Galileo's* pictures revealed the asteroid as a cratered, potato-shaped rock, which is pretty much what astronomers expected asteroids to look like. Gaspra's surface is covered with impact craters. While Gaspra is as old as most other asteroids—4.6 billion years—its surface, judging from the number of small craters, is estimated to be about 200 million years old. Since Gaspra was named for a resort on the Crimean peninsula, many of the asteroid's craters have been named for famous resorts and spas.

Ida had a much bigger surprise in store: It has a satellite! Named Dactyl, it is the first natural satellite of an asteroid ever discovered. (In some mythological accounts, the Dactyli were the children of the nymph Ida and the god Zeus, who was the Greek version of Jupiter.) Dactyl orbits Ida at a distance of approximately 56 miles (90 km). It is about 1 by 0.75 miles (1.6 by 1.2 km) and is surprisingly round for such a small body. (Gravity tends to pull an object into the shape of a sphere, but gravity is also a weak force. If an object is small enough, the material of which it is made is stronger than the gravity it generates. When this happens, the object's gravity is not strong enough to pull it into the shape of a sphere. This is why most small asteroids and moons are not round.)

Ida is part of a group of asteroids called the Koronis family. Because their orbits are so closely related, it is thought that they

The discovery that one out of the first two asteroids observed up close is a **binary system** suggests that double asteroids might be more common than previously suspected. In fact, it is believed that as many as 16 percent of all near-Earth asteroids larger than 66 feet (200 m) may be binary.

The asteroid Gaspra was photographed by the *Galileo* spacecraft. (NASA/JPL)

Ida's moon, Dactyl, is visible as the small dot to the right. Dactyl is only 1 by 0.75 miles (1.6 by 1.2 km) wide and orbits just 56 miles (90 km) from Ida. (NASA/JPL)

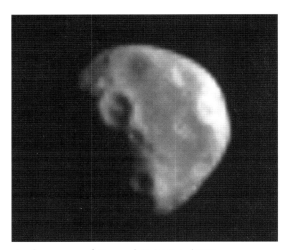

A close-up of Dactyl (NASA/JPL)

are the remnants of a much larger asteroid that was shattered by an impact. Since the composition of Dactyl doesn't exactly match that of Ida, it may be part of the impactor rather than a fragment of the original asteroid.

The *NEAR Shoemaker* spacecraft observed Mathilde in 1997 while on its way to Eros. The most interesting characteristics of Mathilde are its very large craters. At least five craters are larger than 12 miles (20 km) in diameter, while the asteroid itself is only 36.6 by 29.2 miles (59 by 47 km). One hemisphere of Mathilde is scarred by an impact crater so large that scientists don't understand why the asteroid wasn't destroyed by the collision. Neither Ida nor Gaspra have such large craters, and it is a mystery how they were produced on such a small body as Mathilde. Perhaps one explanation is that Mathilde has less mass than scientists expected. Mathilde's density is very low, suggesting that it may be porous, like Styrofoam. This may help account for the large craters, since such a light material would be more able to absorb a powerful impact.

A huge crater on one side of Mathilde was revealed in this photograph taken by the *Galileo* spacecraft. (NASA/JPL)

Gaspra and Ida look very much like Mars's two moons, Phobos and Deimos, giving support to the long-held theory that Phobos and Deimos may have been asteroids captured by Mars's gravity. It is thought that several of the small moons of Jupiter and Saturn are also captured asteroids.

There are other ways to explore asteroids than by using spacecraft. Some astronomers have used radar. By bouncing signals off an asteroid, scientists can determine its shape, size, period of rotation, and other information. Although radar cannot image the same details that a photo can, astronomers can determine something of the nature of the surface by the way different materials reflect the radar beam. The asteroid 216 Kleopatra was explored this way.

Scientists can learn about the shape of many asteroids because most of them rotate as they orbit the Sun. A perfectly spherical asteroid would look pretty much the same all the time, since any one side of it would look like another. Even though it might only appear to be a tiny spot of light in a telescope, astronomers would know that it was of a fairly even shape because its light would remain steady.

An asteroid shaped like a potato, on the other hand, would look very different. If it were rotating so that first its broad side faced Earth and then its narrow end did, the spot of light in the telescope would first look bright, then dim, then bright again. By carefully studying the changes in brightness of a rotating asteroid, scientists can get a very accurate idea of its shape. The elongated peanut shape of the asteroid Eros was discovered in this way. An even stranger asteroid, 624 Hektor, was determined most likely to be two asteroids that orbit so close to each other that they are probably touching!

A Special Asteroid

The *NEAR Shoemaker* spacecraft entered orbit around Eros on Valentine's Day, 2000. *NEAR's* observations gave planetary scientists their best look yet at one of these solar system leftovers, sending back thousands of high-quality photographs as well as other information.

Eros was discovered photographically by Gustav Witt, director of the Urania Observatory, in Berlin, Germany, on Saturday night, August 13, 1898. It was independently photographed on the same night by August H. P. Charlois, of Nice, France. August 14 was a Sunday and the next day was a holiday, so the French planet hunter didn't examine his plate until the 16th, thus losing the honor of being the discoverer. It was named Eros, for the Greek god of love.

As soon as Eros's orbit was calculated, it was clear that something unusual had been found. Up to that time, every asteroid that had been discovered orbited between Mars and Jupiter. Eros, on the other hand, came inside the orbit of Mars. Its average distance from the Sun, 1.458 AU, was actually less than Mars's average distance of 1.524 AU. Eros could come as close to the Sun as 1.133 AU. Since Earth's average distance is 1 AU, Eros can get quite close to us. When Eros makes its closest approach to the Sun at the same time Earth is at its farthest, the asteroid can get as close to Earth as about 0.15 AU (14 million miles). Because of this, Eros is considered to be a near-Earth asteroid.

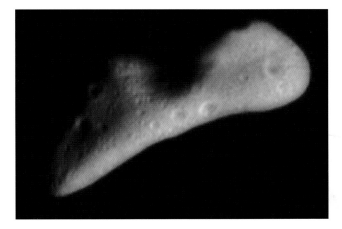

This image of Eros shows not only its true color, but its irregular shape. The deep depression on its upper side is called the "saddle." (NASA/JPL)

Astronomers also noticed that Eros's brightness changes over time, varying over a period of about 5.3 hours. These changes are due to its rotation—once every 5 hours, 16 minutes—which indicates that it must have a very elongated shape. When its long side faces Earth, Eros looks bright. When one of its small ends faces Earth, it looks dimmer. The light variations not only give information on the rotation pole orientation, but also give a fairly good idea of the overall shape. A 1938 estimate found that the brightness variations could be accounted for if Eros had the shape of a cylinder 22 miles (35 km) long, 10 miles (16 km) wide, and 5 miles (8 km) thick, rotating about the shortest axis. The images from the *NEAR* spacecraft proved that while Eros is much more irregular in shape than expected, the early size estimates were pretty close. *NEAR*'s measurements showed that the asteroid is 22 by 8 by 8 miles (33 x 13 x 13 km).

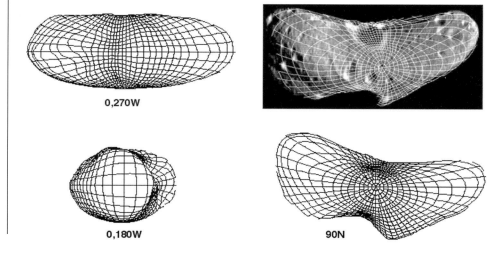

These views of Eros show its highly irregular shape, suggesting that Eros may be the remnant of a much larger body that was shattered by an impact. (NASA/JPL)

Eros is heavily cratered, which means that its surface is not young. Craters have probably accumulated on the surface of Eros for billions of years. (Crater counting is a method commonly used to estimate the ages of surface features on planets and moons.) Without weather on the dry, airless asteroid, there is nothing to erase or erode the ancient scars of impacts. As a result, the surface of Eros is saturated with craters. One strange feature on the asteroid, which was dubbed the "saddle" by NEAR team members (but now officially known as Himeros), is curiously devoid of cratering. Himeros could be a very young dent in the side of Eros created by a large impact.

Another intriguing discovery about Eros is the many boulders on its surface. Hundreds of them are scattered everywhere. They were probably created by **meteor** impacts ejecting material from deep beneath the surface of Eros. Analyzing the boulders will give astronomers an idea of what the interior of Eros is like.

Eros helped solve an ongoing mystery about asteroids. Many were not the right color for the materials scientists thought they were made of. Rocky asteroids were darker and redder than they should be, implying that they had more iron in their makeup than expected. Studying the surface of Eros, American scientist Beth Clark found that this was caused by "space weathering," in which the solar wind slowly evaporates the surface, causing individual grains to be coated with a microscopic film of reddish iron. This ultrathin coating of metal fooled astronomers into thinking the asteroid was made of more iron than it really is.

NEAR Shoemaker ended its mission by gently touching down on Eros in February 2001—the first spacecraft to make a landing

OBSERVING ASTEROIDS

There are no asteroids that can be seen with the naked eye—they can be seen only with telescopes or, rarely, binoculars. Since there are many asteroids that can be observed and they change their positions rapidly, it would be best to check an astronomy magazine for the current positions of the most important asteroids.

To someone standing on one side of the "saddle," the opposite side would seem to rise like a wall straight up into the sky. (NASA/JPL)

(32)

on an asteroid. The gravity on Eros is very weak but enough to hold the *NEAR* spacecraft. A 200-pound (90-kg) person on Earth might weigh about 2 ounces (57 grams) on Eros. A rock thrown from the asteroid's surface at 22 miles (35 km) an hour would escape into space.

Loose boulders on the surface of Eros (NASA/JPL)

For nearly 35 years, Eleanor F. "Glo" Helin has been working for the California Institute of Technology and the Jet Propulsion Laboratory. She is Principal Investigator of the electronic near-Earth asteroid (and comet) search program, which has detected more than 26,000 objects. Before this, she founded the Palomar Observatory's Planet-Crossing Asteroid Survey. This program discovered several thousand asteroids of all types, including almost 30 percent of the known near-Earth asteroids, as well as twenty comets. One of the program's most significant discoveries was that of asteroid 2062 Aten, the first asteroid found to have an orbit smaller than that of Earth. It was the first of a new class of asteroids, now numbering 30.

During the 1980s, Helin organized and coordinated the International Near-Earth Asteroid Survey (INAS), which inspired worldwide interest in asteroids. In recognition of her achievements, she received NASA's Exceptional Service Medal, and asteroid 3267 Helin was named for her.

Helin has also been searching for distant transneptunian objects (TNOs)—bodies orbiting beyond the planet Neptune. In 1996 she and David Rabinowitz discovered the first TNO, called 1996 RQ20. Since then, they have discovered two additional TNOs.

Future plans include more flybys and landings on asteroids, perhaps even by astronauts. Since most asteroids are composed of almost solid metal in a very pure form, there have also been many schemes proposed to "mine" them, bringing valuable metals and minerals back to Earth. The metal in even a small asteroid would be worth many billions of dollars. Asteroid mining has been a staple of science fiction since the 1930s, and it may yet become a reality.

CHAPTER FIVE

DISCOVERING COMETS

The night sky does not change very much—it is reassuringly predictable. There is an occasional eclipse of the Moon and sometimes a shooting star, but all in all the night sky tends to look pretty much the same. This is probably why ancient people became so excited when a comet appeared. It was a very strange, eerie visitor, looking to some people like "a great red dragon," as the Book of Revelation describes it. Other early accounts described comets as resembling dragons in the sky, as well as flaming swords, spears, torches, and other fearful things. The word *comet* itself comes from the Greek word meaning "bearded" or "hairy," because comets look like stars with long streamers of hair flowing behind them.

Whatever their description, everyone agreed that comets foretold death, calamities, and disasters. In the 1450s, Pope Callistus III ordered prayers for deliverance "from the devil, the Turk and the comet." In *Paradise Lost*, the poet John Milton wrote in 1667 that a comet "shakes down diseases, pestilence and war." Actually, fear

A bright comet is a rare but beautiful object in the night sky.

In early times, comets were thought to be omens of doom, war, disease, and disaster.

of comets wasn't limited to ancient people—comets caused panics well into the twentieth century. Even as recently as 1998 some people were predicting worldwide catastrophes based on the appearance of Comet Hale-Bopp.

For a long time, no one knew what comets really were. Most people thought they occurred within Earth's atmosphere, like clouds or **auroras**. It wasn't until 1577 that the Danish astronomer Tycho Brahe deduced that comets were actually more distant than the Moon.

(36)

In 1704, the English astronomer Edmond Halley applied Isaac Newton's recently discovered law of gravity and found that comets traveled in elongated elliptical orbits around the Sun. Calculating the orbits of several well-recorded comets, he found that four of them—the comets of 1456, 1531, 1607, and 1682— had exactly the same orbit and appeared almost exactly at 75-year intervals. He concluded that these were not four different comets but the same one, reappearing over and over again as its orbit carried it around the Sun. Using his data, he predicted that the

A great comet appeared in 1857. This French cartoon illustrated the fears of many people that the comet might hit Earth.

Halley's Comet as it appeared in a telescope during its most recent visit near Earth (NASA)

comet would appear again in 1758. And on Christmas night of that year, the comet returned. It was named Halley's Comet in his honor. (According to modern nomenclature the comet is referred to as "Comet Halley," but most people still refer to it by its historic name of Halley's Comet.)

Today, astronomers have logged nearly 2,000 different comets. All of them are in elliptical orbits around the Sun. Astronomers have divided them into two groups: *long-period comets*, for which the farthest points in their orbits are beyond Pluto, perhaps as far as tens of thousands of AU from the Sun, and *short-period comets*, for which the most distant points in their orbits are within the orbit of Pluto. The latter probably started out as long-period comets, but their orbits were shortened by the gravitational effects of the large outer planets—Jupiter, Saturn, Uranus, and Neptune.

Sir Edmond Halley

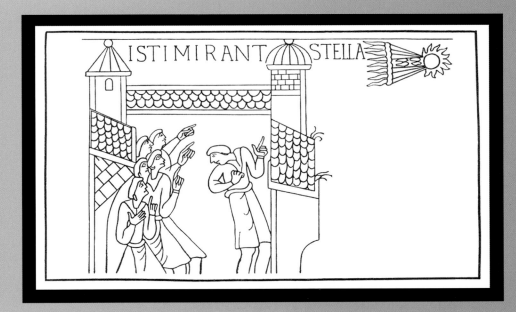

ISTI MIRANT STELLA

The Bayeux Tapestry

Edmond Halley's discovery that comets are objects in orbit around the Sun and that they make regular, predictable appearances helped dispel the myth that they are supernatural portents of evil.

Once astronomers knew the orbit of Halley's Comet, they looked for even earlier records of its appearance. It seems to have been the comet that appeared in A.D. 66, which was associated with the destruction of Jerusalem four years later. Five orbits later, it was linked to the fall of Attila the Hun in 451. In 1066 it appeared in the sky during the Norman conquest of England and is depicted in the famous Bayeux Tapestry, which was created to commemorate the inva-

sion. The American author Mark Twain was very proud that he'd been born in a year, 1835, when Halley's Comet was in the sky—and by a strange coincidence, he died in 1910, the next time the comet came around.

The most recent visit by the comet was in 1986, when millions of people all over the world looked forward to seeing this most famous of all comets (though it was nowhere near as spectacular as it was in 1910, when it came unusually close to Earth). This time, however, it was met by a spacecraft sent from Earth: the *Giotto* probe, which took the first close-up photos of the comet's **nucleus**.

Here Earth and the Moon are seen passing through the tail of a large comet, much as they did in 1910, when the tail of Halley's Comet swept past our planet. So tenuous is the tail of a comet—"the next best thing to nothing at all," as one astronomer put it—that Earth would not be affected at all.

Comets are named after their discoverers, or codiscoverers if two people report the comet at the same time. If the discoverer finds more than one comet, a number is added after its name. Some comet hunters are fortunate enough to discover not just one comet but a great many. For example, Caroline Herschel, sister of William Herschel, the discoverer of Uranus, discovered eight comets between 1786 and 1797. Comet Ikeya-Seki honors two Japanese comet hunters, Kaoru Ikeya and Tsunomu Seki, while Comet Shoemaker-Levy 9 was the ninth comet discovered by the team of Gene Shoemaker, Caroline Shoemaker (who holds the record for having discovered more comets than any other individual, 32 at the last count), and David Levy.

What Are Comets?

In the words of astronomer Fred Whipple, comets are little more than "dirty snowballs"—enormous, drifting icebergs composed of a mixture of ice and sooty dirt, which contain masses of rocks and gravel held together by a "glue" of frozen gases and ice. Most of the comets that have been observed are only 0.5 to 12 miles (1 to 20 km) wide and much too small to be seen with earthbound telescopes. It is not until a comet approaches the Sun and warms up that it can be seen at all.

In the vast deep freeze beyond Pluto, where most comets originate, sunlight is far too weak to provide any warmth, and a comet's ice is frozen as hard as steel. But as a comet comes within about 3 AU of the Sun—about the distance of the main asteroid belt—some of its ice begins to turn to gas. The closer it gets to the Sun, the more of its ice turns to gas. This gas forms a kind of atmosphere around the comet called a **coma**.

As the comet becomes warmer and warmer, the coma grows larger, eventually becoming hundreds and even thousands of miles wide. Meanwhile, the glowing gases begin to form a long, flowing tail. This is also caused by the Sun. Light pressure and the solar wind carry gas and dust away from the coma in a direction away from the Sun. Contrary to appearance, a comet's tail isn't always streaming out behind it. In fact, after the comet has swung around the Sun and is returning to the outer solar system, its tail actually *precedes* the comet.

The tail is usually composed of two parts. There is a curved, yellowish tail called the **dust tail**, since that is what it is mostly

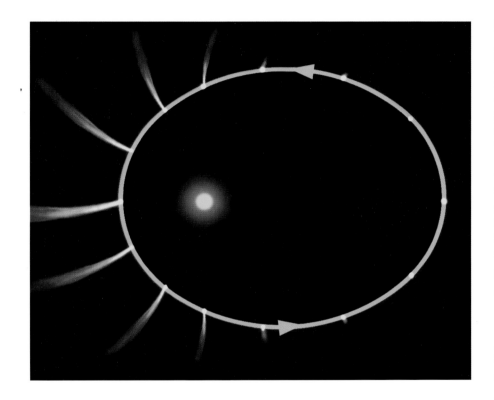

Comets can have very elliptical orbits. As a comet approaches the Sun, it warms up and a tail starts to form. The tail always points away from the Sun, whether the comet is approaching it or receding, as the gases that form the tail are pushed away by the solar wind. The comet's tail does not indicate its direction of motion.

made of. This is usually the brightest tail. The pressure of sunlight against the tiny grains forces the tail away from the Sun. The second, and usually dimmer, tail is the **ion tail** or gas tail. It is caused by particles of the solar wind pushing electrically charged atoms (**ions**) from the coma.

A comet is therefore composed of three parts: a nucleus, which is the dirty iceberg itself; then when the comet nears the

The parts of a typical comet: Even though the coma and tail can be enormous—the tail potentially millions of miles long—the nucleus is a very tiny object only a few miles across, which is too small to be seen at this scale. Earth is shown next to the comet for comparison.

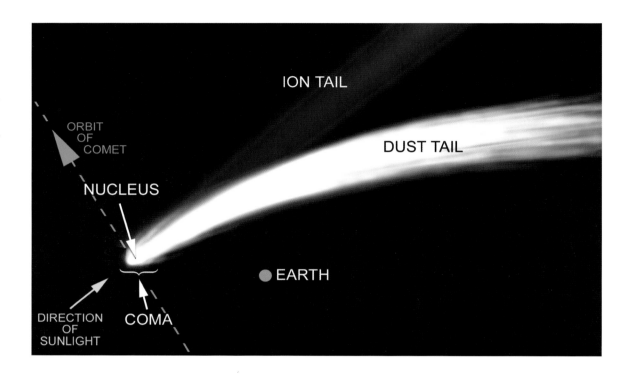

Sun and begins to warm up, a thin, wispy coma, which can grow to be larger than Jupiter; and a vast tail, which can be many millions of miles long.

When the *Giotto* spacecraft flew past the nucleus of Halley's Comet in 1986, it discovered that the nucleus was a black, peanut-shaped object about 9 miles (15 km) long and 5 miles (8 km) wide. The surface is black because of the crust of dark, sooty dirt left behind by the evaporating ice. This crust, which is

(44)

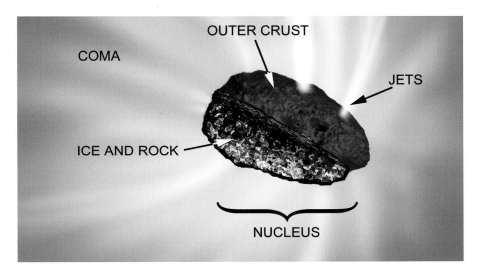

COMA

OUTER CRUST

JETS

ICE AND ROCK

NUCLEUS

The parts of a comet's coma and nucleus

The Italian space probe *Giotto* snapped this close-up of the nucleus of Halley's Comet, revealing the huge jets of gases erupting from the coal-black surface. (NASA)

as black as black velvet, is composed of carbon-rich **organic** compounds.

Huge jets of gas were seen erupting from the nucleus, like gigantic geysers. These shoot off for miles in all directions, but eventually curve back under the pressure of the solar wind. These jets can act like rockets, causing the nucleus to spin erratically.

Every time a comet passes through the inner solar system, it loses a little more of its substance, losing as much as 3 feet (1 m) of its ice as it is evaporated by the Sun. For this reason, a comet has a limited life span. It will eventually lose all of its ice—or at least all of the ice it needs to hold itself together—and it will disintegrate, or fall apart. Many comets have actually been seen breaking up into pieces.

The tortured surface of a typical comet as it enters the inner solar system: As ice evaporates into jets and streamers of gas, the surface is slowly eroded away, leaving hills and mesas where the thicker areas of the dark crust protect the ice beneath.

A comet will eventually lose so much of the ice that holds it together that it will fall apart. This most often happens when the comet comes close enough to a large planet, such as Jupiter, or, as in the case of the comet here, too close to the Sun.

A comet the size of Halley's may last only a few thousand trips around the Sun. A comet can also be broken up when it passes too close to the gravitational field of a large planet, such as Jupiter.

There is also a class of daredevil comets called **sungrazers**. These are comets that orbit very close to the Sun, some so closely that the gravity of the Sun has broken them up and destroyed them. Others have even collided with the Sun itself!

Impact Scar

The orbit of Comet Shoemaker-Levy 9 brought it too close to Jupiter, and the giant planet tore the comet into more than two dozen pieces, which spread out one after the other like beads on a string. (NASA)

A spectacular finale to a comet's life was observed in 1994, when Comet Shoemaker-Levy 9 collided with Jupiter. It had already passed too close to the giant planet in 1992 and was torn into more than 20 smaller pieces by Jupiter's powerful gravity. Swinging into a wide orbit, the fragments looped around Jupiter and finally collided with the planet in July 1994. The impacts were tremendously violent—the pieces struck Jupiter's atmosphere at a speed of 37 miles (60 km) per second—creating titanic **fireballs** that were visible from Earth. The explosions were equivalent to 225,000 megaton nuclear bombs (by comparison, the atomic bomb exploded over Hiroshima, Japan, at the end of World War II was only 12.5 kilotons—18,000 times less powerful than the fragments that hit Jupiter). Long chains of craters on some of Jupiter's moons suggest that impacts such as this have happened often in the past.

Comet Shoemaker-Levy 9 hit Jupiter on the side of the planet that was facing away from Earth, so astronomers were not able to see the actual impacts. However, as the planet rotated, the enormous scars created by the titanic explosions—each larger than Earth itself—came into view. (NASA)

The solar system is surrounded by a vast, spherical cloud of icy bodies called the Oort cloud. This is the source of most long-period comets.

Where Do They Come From?

In the late 1940s, Dutch astronomer Jan Oort wondered about the origin of long-period comets. He noticed that comets' orbits were at all angles to the plane of the solar system—that is, the plane in which most of the planets orbit. This implies the existence of a vast, spherical cloud of comets orbiting far beyond Pluto. It might contain, he calculated, at least 190 billion comets. This cloud, named the **Oort cloud** in 1968 in his honor, may extend as far as 30 trillion miles (48.3 trillion km, 200,000 AU, or 3 light-years) from the Sun! The nearest star to our solar system, Alpha Centauri, is 4.3 light years away, so it can be said that the outer limits of our solar system extend nearly three-quarters of the way to the next star in space.

The Oort cloud is so far from the Sun that gravity has only the most tenuous hold upon the most distant objects in the cloud. These objects are very susceptible to the influence of the stars they pass, which might send one of the icebergs spiraling inward on a long journey toward the Sun. Since the Oort cloud is spherical, surrounding the entire solar system like a globe, long-period comets can fall toward the Sun from any direction.

Short-period comets, however, may have a different source. Most of these comets, unlike their long-period cousins, orbit the Sun close to the plane of the solar system. Irish astronomer Kenneth Edgeworth and Dutch astronomer Gerard Kuiper, working more than half a century ago, suggested the existence of a vast belt of comets surrounding the Sun in near-circular orbits

SOME RETURNING COMETS

COMET	PERIOD	LAST RETURN*	NEXT RETURN*
Encke	3.3 years	2003	2007 (but is always visible through a telescope)
Holmes	7.1 years	2000	2007
Tempel 2	5.3 years	1999	2005
Faye	7.4 years	1998	2006
Halley	76 years	1986	2062

* "Return" refers to when a comet comes into the inner solar system and makes its closest approach to the Sun.

just beyond the orbit of Pluto. This region is usually called the **Kuiper belt**.

Astronomers studying the Kuiper belt realized that there may be very large icy bodies in it—perhaps as large as 0.8 to 1.3 times the mass of Earth. A search began in the late 1980s to find these objects. The first one was discovered in 1992—a tiny, dark object only about 200 miles (320 km) in diameter, orbiting 4.5 AU farther from the Sun than Pluto. By the end of the century, about 60 Kuiper belt objects had been discovered, with about 10 new ones being found every year. Ranging in size from about 60 miles (100 km) to about 472 miles (760 km), these dark, reddish icy bodies

In October 2002 scientists Chad Trujillo and Mike Brown discovered an object they have tentatively named Quaoar. A billion miles farther from the Sun than Pluto, it is the farthest object in the solar system ever to be seen with a telescope. Although only half the size of Pluto, Quaoar is still larger than all of the asteroids combined (though because it is probably made almost entirely of ice, it is not as *massive* as the metal-rich asteroids, so it would only be about a third as massive as all of them combined). Since it orbits in the midst of the Kuiper belt, Quaoar is probably made of ice and dust like the comets that come from that region, although it is about 100 million times larger than any known comet.

Scientists have found more than 500 icy Kuiper belt objects, but until the discovery of Quaoar they have all been significantly smaller than Pluto. The largest one until now was Varuna, which is about 540 miles (900 km) wide. Quaoar is 800 miles (1,300 km) wide. The discovery of such a large object in the Kuiper belt lends credence to the theory that Pluto and its moon Charon may simply be Kuiper belt objects that are orbiting at the innermost edge of the belt.

Quaoar is the largest known Kuiper belt object, an icy body about half the size of Pluto. It orbits at a distance of 42 AU—farther from the Sun than either Neptune or Pluto. From Quaoar's surface the Sun appears only as a bright star 1,764 times dimmer than it looks from the surface of Earth.

resemble Pluto so greatly that most astronomers now think Pluto is really just a large Kuiper belt object orbiting at the innermost edge of the region. Some astronomers estimate that there may be up to 200 million Halley-sized comets—about 6.2 to 12.4 miles (10 to 20 km)—in the belt and maybe as many as 6.7 billion objects at least 1.2 miles (2 km) in size.

Are They Comets — or What?

There are a number of objects that seem to elude exact classification. Are they asteroids or comets? Part of the problem is that when they are not being warmed by the Sun and are not surrounded by brightly glowing gas, comets look just like asteroids. For example, one recently discovered "asteroid" was later found to be an already well-known comet in its inactive phase.

In 1977 astronomer Charles Kowal discovered an asteroid he named Chiron. Although it had a cometlike orbit between Saturn and Uranus, it resembled an ordinary asteroid in every other way—except that it orbited farther from the Sun than any other known asteroid. It had the same dark, blackish color of most asteroids and at 155 miles (250 km) in diameter, it was much larger than any known comet—fifteen times larger than the nucleus of Halley's Comet. But when its orbit brought it closer to that of Saturn, and closer to the Sun, it suddenly began to grow brighter. Soon, other observers began to report seeing Chiron surrounded by a fuzzy cloud of glowing gas. Chiron, to everyone's surprise, was no asteroid after all—it was a comet!

Asteroid, comet, or Kuiper belt object? Chiron, seen here as it passes near the orbit of Saturn, blurs the distinction between these bodies. Although it resembles a large asteroid, it will begin to develop a thin coma as sunlight evaporates its icy surface.

Many scientists now think that Chiron is a Kuiper belt object that—possibly under the influence of one of the giant planets or because of a collision—wandered into the outer solar system, orbiting the Sun closer than any of its companions. In fact, the discovery of Chiron was one of the factors that led astronomers to start thinking about the existence of similar bodies in the region beyond Pluto.

Astronomers began to realize that their old distinctions between asteroids and comets might not be as clear-cut as they had originally thought. There might instead be a gradual blurring from objects that are almost entirely rock and metal to those that are almost entirely ice.

HOW TO DISCOVER A COMET

Most new comets are discovered by amateur astronomers. The best way to go about looking for new comets yourself would be to join a local astronomy club. Almost every city has one. Check with your science teacher or the astronomy department at a nearby university or community college. Even if you don't try to discover your own, it's fun to look at comets. There are always several visible during any year. Only a few of them can be seen with the naked eye—most can been seen only with binoculars or telescopes. Some of these comets are regulars that come back on more or less predictable dates, while others are newly discovered and are being seen for the first time. The astronomy magazines and some of the Web sites listed at the end of this book will tell you which comets, if any, are visible at any particular time. If you do observe a comet, try to make a sketch of what it looks like. If you can observe it over a period of time, record its changing position on a star chart.

CHAPTER SIX

TRACKING METEORS

Although people had been reporting stones falling from the sky for centuries, it took scientists a long time to finally acknowledge that this actually happens. Most scientists thought that meteors were an atmospheric phenomenon. In fact, the word *meteor* comes from a Greek word meaning "high in the air." In 1718, for instance, Edmond Halley dismissed the appearance of a particularly bright meteor as the explosion of inflammable "vapors" in the upper atmosphere. Other scientists thought that meteors might be caused by lightning or rocks thrown off by distant volcanoes. When 300 inhabitants of the French town of Barbotan reported the fall of a meteorite, the Royal Academy of Science said it was nothing but a mere folktale. Eventually, however, evidence began to pile up that was too hard to ignore.

In 1803, when more than 3,000 stones fell on the rooftops of the French village of L'Aigle, a scientist named Jean-Baptiste Biot decided to investigate for himself. In his report to the Royal Academy, he noted that while all the rocks that fell on the village

An illustration of a giant fireball seen over England in 1854 from the book *Meteors* (1874), by William Lackland

were similar in composition, none of them resembled rocks found naturally in the area. The only reasonable conclusion, he said, was that they had in fact fallen from the sky. Still, no one knew how the stones got up in the sky in the first place. It was a complete mystery.

In 1794 two German scientists, Ernst Chladni and Georg Lichtenberg, came up with the remarkable idea that the origin of meteors might be extraterrestrial. Chladni studied the reports of meteorite falls, especially those that had occurred since 1700. He also examined as many different fragments as he could, including a 1,500-pound (680-kg) stony-iron meteorite that had fallen in Siberia in 1749. He eventually eliminated all other possibilities—

such as lightning, volcanoes, atmospheric vapors, hoaxes, etc.—and was left with only one conclusion: Meteorites originated in outer space.

Chladni said that meteors were small masses of iron or stone wandering through space. Every now and then, one or more will encounter Earth's atmosphere, where they suddenly blaze into brilliant visibility. He even went so far as to speculate on the origin of meteorites, suggesting that they might either be the remnants of larger bodies that had exploded or were material that had failed to coalesce into a moon or planet. Since we now know that some meteorites are fragments of shattered asteroids, which in turn are probably material that failed to form into a planet, Chladni's guess was a very good one on both counts. The work of Chladni and others forced scientists to finally accept not only the reality of meteorites but also their extraterrestrial origin.

The Comet Connection

The bright streaks of light we sometimes see in the night sky, which we call "shooting stars," might not seem to have much to do with comets. But there is a very real, and important, connection.

Although meteors can be seen on almost any night of the year, there are certain dates on which dozens and sometimes even hundreds of meteors are visible. Such events are called "meteor showers," and there are at least seven that occur at regular intervals.

In 1866, Giovanni Schiaparelli, the Italian astronomer who had first observed the "canals" of Mars, realized that the Perseid meteor shower, which happens around August 12 every year,

A meteor shower such as the Leonids can be a spectacular sight. The meteors seem to radiate from a central point, but this is only an effect of perspective, just as parallel railroad tracks seem to converge toward the horizon.

Needed:

Cookie sheet
Plastic wrap
Magnet

Piece of paper
Magnifying glass

Line the cookie sheet with the plastic wrap and place it somewhere outdoors where the sky above is unobstructed and the sheet is protected from the wind. Let the sheet stay outdoors for at least a week. When you bring it back indoors, it will be filled with all sorts of debris: leaves, dirt, dead bugs, etc. Carefully run the magnet through this material (a piece of paper wrapped over the end of the magnet will make it easier to remove any particles stuck there). Has anything adhered to the magnet? You will probably find at least a few small particles. These are particles from meteorites that have disintegrated in the upper atmosphere. They stick to the magnet because they contain a lot of iron. Look at them with the magnifying glass (or through a microscope). What do the particles look like? Compare what you see with the images below. Particles that resemble these are probably meteoritic in origin.

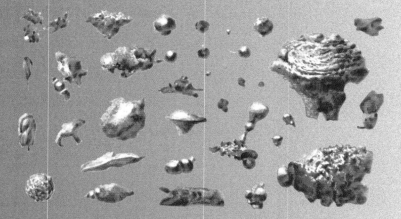

This is a microscopic view of the kinds of meteor fragments and dust that can be collected in your experiment.

occurred whenever Earth crossed the orbit of Comet 1862 III. The Perseid meteors, he said, must be spread out along the orbit of the comet. Soon, the relationships between other comets and regular meteor showers were discovered. Some meteors, astronomers declared, must be tiny bits of debris left behind by the comets themselves.

Most of this debris is very small, ranging from the size of dust motes to grains of sand to peas. When these hit the atmosphere, friction burns them up with a bright flash visible from the ground. Most meteorites are far too small to survive to reach the ground and instead burn up at around 45 to 62 miles (75 to 100 km) above Earth.

Other meteorites are very large and don't burn up quickly. Instead, they leave long, brilliantly flaming trails across the sky. Sometimes they break up or explode. They often can be seen for hundreds of miles around. Very large meteors such as these are called fireballs or **bolides**. Sometimes a large bolide will cause a window-rattling **sonic boom**, like those caused when a fast jet breaks the sound barrier. Occasionally a large meteorite will just skip off Earth's atmosphere—like a stone skipping over the surface of a pond—and continue on its way into space.

Meteor Craters

Every now and then a meteorite is large enough to reach the ground. A meteorite can hit Earth at speeds of 25,000 to 75,000 miles (40,233 to 120,700 km) an hour—up to a hundred times faster than the speed of sound. When a rock larger than 350 tons

Brilliant, long-lasting meteors are called fire-balls or bolides. They are often bright enough to be seen in the daytime, as was this one, which was observed from Washington, D.C., all the way to eastern Pennsylvania.

On any average night, you might see about three meteors an hour before midnight and about fifteen an hour after midnight. But during certain times of the year you may see a meteor shower of sixty or more an hour and, on rare occasions, even hundreds or thousands. Even more rarely you might see a fireball. Though fireballs are more likely to occur during a meteor shower, they can occur at any time of the year. They are often bright enough to be seen in daylight. Almost every regular meteor shower is associated with a past or present comet.

The name of a meteor shower refers to the constellation the meteors appear to come from. They don't really come from *any* constellation, however—that's just an effect of perspective. For example, the Leonids appear to come from the part of the sky in the direction of the constellation Leo.

Here is a chart of some of the best-known meteor showers. The dates are approximate. It would be best to consult a newspaper or astronomy magazine to find out what the exact predicted peak night would be where you live.

Shower Name	Constellation	Date of Maximum Activity	Duration	Average number of meteors
Lyrid	Lyra	April 21, morning	4 days	8 per hour
Perseid	Perseus	August 12, morning	25 days	70 per hour
Orionid	Orion	October 21, morning	14 days	20 per hour
Taurid	Taurus	November 7, midnight	variable	15 per hour
Leonid	Leo	November 16, morning	7 days	20 per hour
Geminid	Gemini	December 12, morning	5.2 days	50 per hour

hits at these speeds, it will explode. When it does, it creates a roughly circular crater. Meteor craters on Earth were once thought to be extremely rare and perhaps even nonexistent. In fact, the best-known of them all, mile-wide Meteor Crater, in Arizona, was long thought to be a volcanic feature. It was only through the tireless efforts of one scientist, Daniel Barringer, that the true origin of

Meteor Crater was finally accepted. Now more than 150 terrestrial meteor craters have been recognized, ranging in size from just a few hundred feet to 85 miles (137 km) and more.

Comparing photos of Earth seen from space with photos of other worlds such as Mars, the Moon, and the satellites of Jupiter, one is struck by the apparent absence of craters on our planet. Mars, for example, is covered with thousands of craters, some of them hundreds of miles wide. Does this mean that Earth was somehow spared this bombardment? There are several reasons that meteor craters are so hard to find on Earth.

One reason is that Earth is very active geologically. Volcanoes bury thousands of square miles in lava, for instance. The surface of Earth is also constantly being recycled as its continental plates drift around, so that very old craters may be destroyed entirely.

Meteor Crater is a hole half a mile (0.8 km) wide blasted by a meteorite in the Arizona desert 20,000 years ago. (Lunar and Planetary Institute)

Astronomers recently came to a startling conclusion about eight meteorites that had been puzzling them since the 1970s. These meteorites appeared to be relatively young. Atomic dating techniques showed that they were only 1.3 billion years old, where almost all other meteorites found on Earth are the same age as the solar system, about 4.6 billion years old. They also showed signs of melting and **recrystallization** that normally could take place only on a geologically active planet.

With these clues, scientists decided that the meteorites must have been blown off another planet, perhaps by a giant asteroid impact. They eliminated Mercury, since anything blown from it would remain in orbit around the Sun, and they eliminated Venus, since its higher gravity and dense atmosphere would prevent material from being easily blown into space. The outer planets—Jupiter and Saturn—were eliminated because they are made almost entirely of gas and liquid.

The astronomers concluded that the mysterious meteorites must have come from the planet Mars. The gravity on Mars is low enough that a large impact might easily blow material into space. Its atmosphere is thin so it would not be an impediment to material being blown away, and it was geologically active in the past. What really convinced the astronomers was the presence of gases in tiny bubbles inside the meteorite. The composition of these gases matched the composition of Mars's atmosphere. Recently, some scientists have claimed to have found signs of fossilized life forms in the Martian meteorites, a conclusion that has been hotly debated.

And there is the effect of erosion, caused by water, weather, and plant life. These tend to erase craters over long periods of time. The remnants of even a very large crater might be entirely invisible from ground level. Most terrestrial craters have been discovered from the air or in photos taken from astronauts in orbit.

Because of the effects of erosion, there is rarely an easily identifiable crater, so scientists have to look for other signs of an impact. Meteorite fragments are found only at the smallest craters. The heat created by the impact of larger meteorites melts and vaporizes rocks, soil, and meteorite. Scientists therefore look for a special variety of deformed rocks and minerals. Since these can be created only by extreme shock pressures, they are sure signs of an impact origin. One example of this is conical fractures known as **shatter cones**. Other signs include the occurrence of various glasses and high-pressure minerals, as well as rocks melted by the intense heat of impact.

Scientists have identified 160 impact features on Earth, with more being discovered every year. Some of the best-known features include the Wolfe Creek crater in Australia, which is 0.544 mile (0.875 kilometer) wide; Aurounga crater in Africa, an ancient scar 10.2 miles (17 km) across; and the Manicouagan feature in Quebec, a ring-shaped lake 62 miles (100 km) wide.

Impact!

Most meteorites that land on Earth are slowed so much by the atmosphere that they simply land with a thud, as though they'd been dropped from a high-flying airplane. Cars, houses, and even

people have been hit by falling meteorites, though the chances of this happening to you are too rare to bother worrying about. One scientist calculated that the chances of being hit by a meteorite are about the same as being hit by a fish dropped by a passing eagle.

The heaviest bombardment of impacts occurred during the early formation of Earth, since the solar system was still filled with debris left over from its formation. As Earth and the other planets swept up this material, giant impacts grew rarer. The asteroid impact that may have wiped out the dinosaurs occurred 65 mil–

The dots on this map show the locations of most of the known impact craters on Earth. Because of erosion and vegetation, most of these were not discovered until it was possible to study photos taken by high-flying aircraft and astronauts. Most of the craters that have been discovered so far are on very ancient terrain that has not changed much over billions of years.

Sixty-five million years ago a rock 6 to 12 miles (19 to 20 km) wide hit Earth near the coast of present-day Yucatán. The trillion-ton missile blasted a crater 105 miles (170 km) wide. Tidal waves thousands of feet high swept outward at up to 450 miles (724 km) an hour, scouring the earth beneath. Meanwhile, debris from the explosion, in the form of millions of blazing meteorites, fell all over Earth, igniting worldwide forest fires. Billions of tons of dust and water vapor were blown into the upper atmosphere, to say nothing of smoke from the forest fires, plunging Earth into darkness for up to a year.

Deprived of sunlight, plants died. Animals that depended on plants for food died, and, in turn, animals that ate plant-eaters died. Nearly 70 percent of all species then living on Earth vanished after the impact.

Oddly enough, while an impact may have spelled the end of the dinosaurs, they may also have owed their existence to an even earlier impact. According to a recent theory, an asteroid hit Earth 200 million years ago and killed off various species. Consequently, there were fewer animals left to compete for food. The resulting increased food supply allowed the dinosaurs to flourish and eventually dominate the planet.

lion years ago, while the Arizona meteor crater was created 20,000 to 40,000 years ago, long before any human beings existed in North America to observe the event, but this doesn't mean that impacts don't still occur today.

One of the most violent events to occur in modern times took place in the region of the Tunguska River in Siberia in 1908. On the cold, clear morning of June 30, thousands of people who lived in the region witnessed a huge ball of fire cross the sky, followed by a series of tremendous explosions. These were so loud they were heard 600 miles (965 km) away. One hundred to 150 miles (160 to 241 km) from the impact, men and horses were blown over and some people were knocked unconscious. Fires started in the forests, and herds of reindeer were killed. Enormous waves rushed down the river, and houses and walls collapsed. From a distance of 250 miles (402 km) a jet of flame was seen spurting into the sky, reaching a height of at least 12 miles (19 km). Shocks, like those from an earthquake, were recorded as far away as 600 miles (1,000 km).

What happened that morning in Siberia? The event occurred in one of the most remote, inaccessible regions in the world. It was not until 1927 that an expedition finally reached the area to find out. The scientists were shocked at what they saw, even after the passage of nearly 20 years. The forest in an area more than 60 miles (97 km) in diameter had been blasted completely flat. Not a tree was left standing—they were all destroyed, flattened, and charred. The scientists were certain that some cosmic visitor had exploded over Siberia—but what was it? The strangest aspect was the lack of a crater.

In 1908 either the core of a comet or a small asteroid exploded in the air above a northern Siberian forest. The tremendous blast flattened thousands of trees and knocked people down many miles away.

When the Russian expedition was finally able to reach the site of the Tunguska blast in Siberia, they were astonished to see thousands of trees still flattened to the ground. (NASA)

Whatever it was must have exploded high in the air, before it ever reached the ground. There have been a great many theories in the 75 years since—ranging from UFOs to black holes—but the most likely explanation is that Earth was hit by a large, stony meteorite that exploded at an altitude of about 6 miles (9.7 km). It's been estimated that the object was between 98 and 197 feet (30 and 60 m) wide and exploded with the force of an H-bomb.

If the object had struck just a little less than five hours earlier it would have hit the city of St. Petersburg . . . with consequences that would be horrible to imagine. Today—inspired in large part by the collision of Comet Shoemaker-Levy 9 with Jupiter and the strong evidence that an asteroid impact killed off the dinosaurs—astronomers and other scientists take the possibility of another large-scale impact very seriously. Even a relatively small meteorite, such as the one that hit Siberia, could wipe out a city.

Many astronomers and other scientists have tried to interest governments in the potential danger of an asteroid impact—and with some success. Ongoing research is taking place in the United States, Australia, Japan, and throughout Europe.

Impact Hazard

How worried should we be about the possibility of an impact by a large meteorite or asteroid? None of the asteroids or comets we know about are on a collision course with Earth. On the other hand, there undoubtedly are many asteroids that have not yet been discovered. It's possible that one of these could hit at any time, but statistically the chances are very small.

Earth's atmosphere protects it from most near-Earth objects (NEOs) smaller than a medium-sized building, about 160 feet (50 m) in diameter. But if such an object were to reach the ground it would explode with the energy of about 5 megatons—more than enough to destroy an entire city. This is about the size of the object that hit northern Siberia in 1908. Astronomers have calculated that such an object collides with Earth every 300 years. Fortunately, since Earth is covered mostly by water, there is a 70 percent chance of the asteroid landing in an ocean.

From about 160 feet (50 m) up to a diameter of about 0.6 mile (1 km), an NEO could do tremendous damage on a local scale. Above a diameter of about 1.25 miles (2 km), an impacting asteroid would produce severe damage on a global scale. The effect on the environment would be the start of an "impact winter," with loss of crops worldwide and subsequent starvation and disease. Still larger impacts could cause mass extinctions, like the one that ended the age of the dinosaurs 65 million years ago.

So what are the chances of something like this happening now? The minimum impact needed to cause a global catastrophe occurs about once every 500,000 years. Assuming that a quarter of the world's human population would perish if that happened, chances of dying in such an event during the coming year are 1 in 2 million. For comparison, chances of being killed in a car accident within the next year are about 1 in 5,000.

The Future

Once upon a time, asteroids, comets, and meteors were considered the rubbish of the solar system, interesting as curiosities at best and nuisances at worst. Now we know they are as interesting as the planets and moons—and perhaps no less important. For instance, we are now more aware of the—literal—impact these objects have had on Earth, and may have on the future of our planet. An international effort is under way to detect asteroids that may threaten us, though no one yet has any workable idea of what to do in the case of an impending collision. A much more likely impact on the future will be the effect of the exploration and exploitation of the asteroids. They are rich in iron, nickel, and

It may be possible—and profitable—in the future to mine asteroids for the very pure metals of which many of them are formed. (Bonestell Space Art)

other metals that would go a long way toward supplanting the diminishing resources of our planet. And comets, those strange, ghostly visitors from interstellar space may hold the secrets of the origin of the solar system itself.

accretion: accumulation of dust and gas into larger bodies such as stars, planets, and moons.

asteroid: a medium-sized rocky object orbiting the Sun; smaller than a planet, larger than a meteoroid. Also called planetoids or minor planets.

asteroid belt: a region between the orbits of Mars and Jupiter that contains a large number of asteroids.

astronomical unit (AU): the distance of Earth from the Sun, about 93 million miles (153 million km).

aurora: glowing lights seen in the sky of the polar regions on Earth (and some other planets), which are caused by the interaction between electrical particles from the Sun and gases in the upper atmosphere.

binary system: two bodies (such as stars, asteroids, or planets) that orbit around a common center of gravity.

bolide: a fireball large enough to cause a sonic boom.

carbon: an element commonly occurring as coal, graphite, and diamonds; it is an important part of all organic molecules.

carbonate: a compound containing carbon and oxygen.

coma: the glowing envelope of gas and dust immediately surrounding the nucleus of a comet.

comet: a medium-sized icy body orbiting the Sun that's smaller than a planet.

contraction: the process by which a body becomes smaller and denser due to the pull of its own gravity.

crater: a hole of any size created in a body by the impact of a meteor, asteroid, or comet.

differentiation: any process by which materials are separated from their original mixed state and concentrated in different regions.

(73)

dust tail: the part of a comet's tail that is composed mostly of dust.

ecliptic: the plane of Earth's orbit; approximately the plane of the solar system

elliptical: having a shape resembling an ellipse (oval).

fireball: a very large meteor, often bright enough to be seen in the daytime (*also see* bolide).

ion: an electrically charged atom or molecule.

ion tail: the part of a comet's tail that is composed mostly of ionized gas; also called gas tail.

Kirkwood gaps: gaps in the asteroid belt caused by the gravitational effect of Jupiter.

Kuiper belt: a disk-shaped region beyond the orbit of Neptune containing many small icy bodies. It is considered to be the source of the short-period comets.

Lagrangian point: one of five stable positions in a planet's orbit (*also see* Trojan asteroids).

metamorphic rocks: rocks that transform from one type to another.

meteor: a bright streak of light in the sky caused by the entry into Earth's atmosphere of a meteoroid or a small icy particle. Also called a shooting star or falling star.

meteorite: a rock of extraterrestrial origin found on Earth.

meteoroid: a small rocky object orbiting the Sun, smaller than an asteroid.

nucleus: the small, dark solid body within the coma of a comet.

Oort cloud: a vast, approximately spherical cloud of icy bodies that surround the solar system.

organic: denoting molecules and compounds that contain carbon.

planetesimal: a small, asteroid-sized body that accretes into a large, planet-sized body.

protoplanet: a planet at an early stage in its formation.

protoplanetary disk: a large disk of dust and gas that eventually accretes to form planets.

protostar: a sphere of gas that has collapsed far enough to become hot but not yet hot enough to start the process of nuclear fusion.

recrystallization: the process by which a crystalline substance is melted and reforms into a crystal upon cooling.

shatter cone: a small, cone-shaped feature created in a rock by the force of an impact.

silicate: a compound containing silicon and oxygen; for example, ordinary sand.

solar wind: the outrushing gas from the Sun that reaches as far as Earth and even beyond the outer planets.

sonic boom: the sound created by the shock wave of an aircraft or large meteor traveling faster than the speed of sound.

star: a gaseous body massive enough to have triggered nuclear reactions in its interior.

sungrazer: a comet that makes especially close approaches to the Sun.

Trojan asteroids: asteroids orbiting in the Lagrangian points of Jupiter's orbit.

Books

Beatty, J. Kelly, Carolyn Collins Petersen, and Andrew Chaikin, eds. *The New Solar System.* Cambridge, MA: Sky Publishing, 1999.

Bell, Jim, and Jacqueline Mitton. *Asteroid Rendezvous: NEAR Shoemaker's Adventures at Eros.* London: Cambridge University Press, 2002.

Bortz, Alfred B., and Fred Bortz. *Collision Course: Cosmic Impacts and Life on Earth.* Brookfield, CT: The Millbrook Press, 2001.

Gallant, Roy A. *Comets, Asteroids and Meteorites.* Tarrytown, NY: Benchmark Books, 2000.

Hartmann, William K. *Moons and Planets.* Belmont, CA: Wadsworth Publishing, 1999.

Miller, Ron, and William K. Hartmann. *The Grand Tour.* New York: Workman Publishing, 1993.

Norton, O. Richard, and Dorothy S. Norton. *Rocks from Space: Meteorites and Meteorite Hunters.* Missoula, MT: Mountain Press, 1998.

Scagell, Robine. *The New Book of Space.* Brookfield, CT: Copper Beech, 1997.

Schaaf, Fred. *Planetology: Comparing Other Worlds to Our Own.* Danbury, CT: Franklin Watts, 1996.

Spangenburg, Ray, and Kit Moser. *If an Asteroid Hit Earth.* Danbury, CT: Franklin Watts, 2000.

Spencer, John R., and Jacqueline Mitton. *The Great Comet Crash: The Collision of Comet Shoemaker-Levy 9 and Jupiter.* London: Cambridge University Press, 1995.

Magazines

Astronomy
www.astronomy.com

Sky & Telescope
www.skypub.com

Organizations

American Astronomical Society
2000 Florida Avenue NW, Suite 400
Washington, D.C. 20009-1231
www.AAS.org

Association of Lunar and Planetary
  Observers
PO Box 171302
Memphis, TN 38187-1302
www.lpl.arizona.edu/alpo/

Astronomical Society of the Pacific
390 Ashton Avenue
San Francisco, CA 94112
www.astrosociety.org

The Planetary Society
65 N. Catalina Avenue
Pasadena, CA 91106
planetary.org

Web Sites

Alpha Centauri's Universe
www.to-scorpio.com/index.htm
A good site for basic information about
the solar system.

Comet Observation Home Page
encke.jpl.nasa.gov/
All about comets and where to look
for them.

Comets & Meteor Showers
comets.amsmeteors.org/
An excellent guide for observing
comets and meteors, with calendars and
observing tips.

Main Asteroid Belt
www.solstation.com/stars/asteroid.htm
A site devoted to asteroids, the asteroid
belt, the Kuiper belt, and many other
solar system topics.

Minor Planet Names: Alphabetical List
cfa-www.harvard.edu/iau/lists/
MPNames.html
A list of all the named asteroids.

NASA Spacelink
spacelink.msfc.nasa.gov/index.html
Gateway to many NASA Web sites
about the Sun and planets.

The Nine Planets: A Multimedia Tour
of the Solar System
www.nineplanets.org
Detailed information about the Sun,
the planets, and all the moons, including many photos and useful links to
other Web sites.

Solar System Simulator
space.jpl.nasa.gov/
An amazing Web site that allows visitors to travel to all the planets and
moons and create their own views of
these distant worlds.

Space.com
www.space.com
Contains a lot of information about
asteroids, as well as links to other sites.

Terrestrial Impact Craters
www.solarviews.com/eng/tercrate.htm
A Web site devoted to impact craters
on Earth.

Hugo Award–winner Ron Miller is an illustrator and author who specializes in astronomy. He has created or contributed to many books on the subject, including *Cycles of Fire*, *The History of Earth*, and *The Grand Tour*. Among his nonfiction books for young people are *The History of Rockets* and *The History of Science Fiction*, as well as the Worlds Beyond series, which was awarded the 2003 American Institute of Physics Science Writing Award in Physics and Astronomy (Children's) for the first four books—*Extrasolar Planets*, *The Sun*, *Jupiter*, and *Venus*. Miller's work has won many awards and distinctions, including the 2002 Hugo Award for Best Non-Fiction for *The Art of Chesley Bonestell*. He has designed a set of ten commemorative stamps on the planets in our solar system for the U.S. Postal Service. He has written several novels and has worked on a number of science fiction films, such as *Dune* and *Total Recall*. His original paintings can be found in collections all over the world, including that of the National Air and Space Museum in Washington, D.C., and magazines such as *National Geographic*, *Scientific American*, *Sky and Telescope*, and *Natural History*. Miller lives in King George, Virginia, with his wife and cats.